The Beauty In Us-Our Reality

Thanks for
your support!
—nelson
Brown

The Beauty In Us-Our Reality

Printed and Bound in the United States of America
The book is set in Times New Roman.
Designed By Mary Barrows

Cover image used under license from Shutterstock.com
Brick Texture by Vladitto

ISBN-13: 978-1718751903

For More Information:
brownnelsone@gmail.com

Follow me on my Amazon Author Page-Nelson E. Brown

The Beauty In Us-Our Reality

Written By Nelson E. Brown

~ ACKNOWLEDGEMENTS ~

There I was, waiting to take my placement test with the hopes of achieving a score that was high enough for me to secure a spot into one of the top magnet schools in the nation. A few months later, I stood there, shocked to find out that I had the score I needed to gain acceptance into the program of my dreams.

I would like to thank God and all of my friends, relatives, and colleagues who have supported me in all of my endeavors. I never thought that I would be fortunate enough to share my story with individuals who have crossed paths with me as well as ones that have not. Most importantly, I would like to thank my mother, Lisa, and daycare providers, Mr. and Mrs. Boone, who have been my rocks since the day I was born. They are a part of the reason why I had a great childhood, why I am so driven and motivated to get up and go every morning, and why I did not give up when I had so many naysayers who underestimated me and my ability to do great things. They never doubted me. With every math test, with every sports game, and at every awards ceremony of some sort, their presence and enthusiasm said it all. We are some of the people who recognize children as unique individuals who have the power to make a difference in this rapidly changing world. We are the future and we have the ability to march to the beat of our own drums, create the dance moves to our own dances, and sing our own songs with our own lyrics.

TABLE OF CONTENTS

Introduction

We always discuss controversial topics regarding body image and acceptance, but often it is heard from a female's point of view. You rarely hear any males speaking out about their struggles with their body image and self-esteem. Society believes in many stereotypes in men, such as them being unemotional creatures, saying that they are never unsatisfied with their body image/physical appearance. Why are there so many double standards between boys and girls? The insecurities I have about myself in regards to my physical appearance left me with questions, such as why do I feel unattractive. Why don't I have "the look"? How is it possible? I loved everyone else but myself? People have made constant efforts to help me boost my self-confidence, but I was stuck in a rut for my entire life. The academics were on point, but my physical health was pushed on the back burner. I moved further and further into an unhealthy state to the point when I wasted some of my most precious years holding back who I am. Letting things I could not control bother me or trying to fix something that is unfixable are only a few examples. It was not until I decided to make a lifelong lifestyle change through the proper diet and exercise. I am a young man of character, a young man of strength, and one of class. This story is set in my hometown of Randallstown outside of Baltimore. Growing up was filled with so much joy, laughter, and entertainment for me, but many of my family members, friends, and those on the outside looking in don't know about many of the challenges I have faced during these times while I grew up about my body image and searching for self-acceptance. As you take a glimpse of reading this autobiography, you will begin to recognize who I truly am and how I feel outside of any social setting, whether it is in school, at work, or anywhere in this community. Never judge a book by its cover and never underestimate another person because of how they may appear. This is a story of how I lost 70lbs in high school after feeling uncomfortable in my own skin my entire life.

CHAPTER ONE

JUST GETTING STARTED

In the summer before my first year of school in 2004, I entered into school at the age of five not knowing what to expect on the morning of a chilly fall day sitting in the back of my mom's white car. I was dressed in a forest green sweater and light grey sweatpants as I entered that little white house behind silver gates next to the tall tree. Feelings of excitement and nervousness were hidden inside of me when I met my teacher and other 1999 babies in my class.

The first school I attended was where my educational foundation started. That was my first time being away from daycare with children in diapers wearing bibs and sucking on pacifiers between the ages of 2 months and 5 years old. Even though I learned earlier than usual, all of them taught me more of the basic skills that a kid in their first five years of life should learn, such as numbers, colors, the alphabet, shapes, and so much more. All I remember about being in my early childhood class is writing and tracing books and books of cursive letters time after time in a room with a desktop computer, small wooden tables, and my pencil case that contained markers, crayons, pencils, and baby scissors for my pint sized hands. I even had to use a stress ball for my hands to get a better grip whenever I needed to use a writing utensil. I cried because I had never written extensively like that before.

One observation my mom made in this class was that I had the tendency to draw and color everything black. I remember doing that, but I guess it represents the way I felt about the relationship I had with my father figure that was dwindling away.

When you are five years old, you yearn the attention from your mom and a father figure, not just your mom. It breaks my heart when I watch TV and see people my age being misguided, not having anyone to look up to or come to whenever they need help or if they are in trouble. The kids in this predicament blame themselves for his absence, thinking that it is their fault, but I am here to tell them that it is absolutely, NOT. 99% of the time, dad struggled with issues before you entered into this world. Forgiving him is for you and you will feel better. I know it is hard, I struggled with the same thing, but it turns out that I made great childhood memories.

In addition to my very first graduation, the field trip to the zoo was memorable. That was one of my first encounters with a horse, pig, cow, goat, and chicken on a farm with a big red barn near a tractor down a muddy road filled with pumpkins we rode through as a class. They seemed to be very receptive to me once I fed them. I still remember that little brown horse I rode. It actually had me feeling like a cowboy for a short period living the southern lifestyle. Riding that horse gave me a boost of confidence. It created a moment where I did not concern myself with anyone or anything, but me. My weight was not even a thought yet.

In my first year of elementary school, I completed my first project on the country, Greece. I received tons of assistance from my mom in order to get this done because I was eager to do well on it. I had never completed a long-term assignment and wanted to win first prize against my other classmates. This marked my first time I felt like I appreciated something I worked for and earned. Even though I won fourth place instead of first place, a round of applause was given to me by everyone for all of the hard work I put forth into finishing the assignment. The golden trophy that was given to me was designed in the bright, bold numbers (2005) and had a man standing tall with a graduation cap and tassel in his hand. My mom instilled in me that "-hard work pays off-". This was when I figured that out after looking at the trophy, but I was still unsatisfied.

I took my first class picture with my class on our last day of kindergarten. As I look at that picture a decade later, I now see how I looked in the photo kneeling down to the ground, with a frown, and white background. I recall feeling sad minutes before the time came and became uninterested in taking the picture. My mother, feeling sentimental, was willing to savor the moment while I was there. After all the commencement exercises were finished and over with, my friends and I, sadly, went our separate ways. The chapter of our lives at this school ended,however, interactive CDs and games were given to me by my teacher to play on the computer. Many cartoon heroes of mine in these interactive games sharpened my skills for the next stage in education.

Now, I was one of the tallest members of my class who stood out because of his height. Now, unbelievably, I was that chunky kid. People back then gave me backhanded compliments and very abrasive insults. By the next fall and spring, I decided to join a local football and baseball team for another town in the county. Although I do not consider myself a sports fanatic, I do not mind watching sports outside of the ones I have played. You have already been given a taste of my school and social life in the first five years of my existence. I was not equipped or in shape, I was not slim like the other kids and this was the first time people called me chubby, but I was still eager to try something new.

CHAPTER TWO

THE STAR OF THE SHOW

After completing the registration process for football and baseball, I was happy to have had the opportunity to meet the head coach of both teams for this town. The coach assigned me the position of linebacker. My height and weight matched the requirements for that role.

I, today, am glad to have had that experience and football has been my favorite sport ever since. Being five and six years old brought out the curiosity in me. A safety on my favorite football team that I idolized and still idolize to this day is one I admire so much because it seemed as though he was one of the most passionate players on the team I loved with the most heart. I have jerseys, rookie cards, a room painted with the team colors, and a picture of their team's stadium. As you can see, I am a die-hard fan.

Back on the field, I lived up to my idol and tore my opponents to pieces, not literally, of course. It just came to me naturally after many nights of practice swinging the baseball bat and catching the ball in the evenings outside the gates of the sandy baseball field with the father figure in my life the summer before I signed up for sports. He was a sports prodigy, but had his own relationship with basketball. As an inspiring coach for basketball, he knew facts about every player in the league.

My baseball career with this coach was not as successful as my football career, but it was filled with as much entertainment. Unlike our baseball team, the football season ended in an undefeated season, 8-0. Our baseball team had a record that was not even close. I was a shortstop with a decent hand. I hit that ball as far as I could across the sandy brown, diamond shaped field, but would not run as fast. I remember my mom and teammates' parents cheering me on, encouraging me to run to home base.

When my career in these sports ended between the ages of five and seven, I was beginning to adjust to a new school and atmosphere. The presence of the father figure in my life began to fizzle out once he moved further into his alcoholism and as a victim to his addiction. I started attending my second school, another private school around the outskirts of my old school. Meanwhile, my father figure continued to spend that spare time with the little boy he called his son. We rode bikes, shopped at stores, and went to a train station to see trains, which became a new passion of mine.

I developed my passion for trains once I started watching another TV program. Two of the characters were my childhood heroes along with the cartoon characters in other franchises I mentioned earlier. To be honest, I loved two of them because they displayed the best work ethics out of all the other engines. They were meant to be stars. The two of them had a personality and traits that were similar to mine, which made it easy for me to relate to them.

About a year and a half later, I retired from being one of the town's junior league players. I have no clue what happened to them, but I hung up my red, grey, and white jerseys somewhere. I soon joined a gymnastics team in another town. Even though it appeared as though I had fun on the outside, I was always apprehensive about flipping, twisting, and turning in front of the other kids because of my size. No one was there except my mother.

Driving to the gymnastics center almost an hour away, listening to the radio in the backseat, I talked to my mom about what I was going to do even though neither of us had a clue. We arrived there and dispersed. I went to the dressing room to change into some shorts and a shirt as I entered the gym while she ordered some refreshments for herself. Stretching across the blue carpet, watching the ladies dance in their pink leotards and slippers,and watching the other boys in my class do back flips on the balance beams and trampolines made me feel incomplete. Seeing how scrawny the other boys were made my stomach turn as I crumbled to pieces on the inside feeling there was no room for a chubby kid on a gymnastics team. My mother waved through the window of the waiting room every time as I continued to see an empty chair next to her.

CHAPTER THREE

MY FAMILY'S AFFAIRS

The crucial values of being independent, getting an education, and faith were instilled in me by my mom. One of my loved ones is like my mom and has been an important part of my life. She would pick me up from day care, allow me to spend the night at her house, and would often grease my face with Vaseline to protect me from the cold weather. Just being there and being supportive is the reason why I appreciate her role in my life.

I can just imagine how hard it is to care for, nurture, and educate any child nowadays, but one relative of mine is my inspiration as a parent. He is the best dad I have ever seen. Like me, his father was absent for the majority of his life and he does not have a career as a doctor, lawyer, or engineer and he does not have four to five degrees behind his name. However, he breaks his back and jumps through hoops for his kids and is rich because of the love he has for his children and the care he has for them, not because of his ability to have children. It is still early, but if I decide to have a child, I will keep the relationship he has with his children as a blueprint.

My father figure and I share good memories for about the first five years of my life. It was good for a while, but because of his alcoholism, he started spending more time with his long list of liabilities instead of one of his priorities(me). I have awesome memories of my great grandmother who recently passed away from natural causes at the age of eighty-seven. She was a continued support for birthdays and holidays. We even spent some Saturday mornings at bible study at her place of worship. She and I have shared some awesome memories.

After the death of my great grandmother, I saw him for the first time in six years, towards the end of my senior year of high school. He had since been diagnosed with epilepsy and is disabled. Even after what has transpired between us, I do not wish anything bad to happen to him. Of course, I wish he would have been more consistent in my life, but sometimes I think his absence was for the best. I have other males and other females who have influenced me in positive ways. They have instilled many values and principles in me throughout the years.

Family feuds arise all the time in any family. Whether it is sibling rivalry, drug addiction, substance abuse, neglect, you name it. NOBODY IS PERFECT! We all have our problems, but we love and care for each other. Watching each other grow generation after generation is what keeps us together. Sometimes loving someone from a distance is for the best. I do not hate the father figure in my life for who he is, I dislike the decisions he has made for my mother, himself, and me. Life could have been so much better for him, but for everything we do, there is a consequence, good or bad.

With my mom and other loved ones by my side, I remained precocious at this new private school. I know that some friends were out of the picture, but I made three new friends. We all met and hung out with each other for the next three years.

CHAPTER FOUR

MY FIRST TRANSITION

Here I am at six years old. A new dawn, new day, and a new year came in the next school year. My teacher was my permanent teacher for the next year at a new private Christian school.

Traditions at this school included religious ceremonies, classes, and commencement exercises. At these events, every student from the school was a toddler or an adolescent and would come out to participate in the religiously educational program. The guitarist on the second floor would play her wooden baby while we all would sing along. Her students (the older students) would dress in white robes and light the candles, but eventually went along. This was no surprise to me because I was accustomed to attending church at a very young age. I was afforded the opportunity to purchase and use the bible in and outside of school. The chapel was covered with brown pews, blue rugs, and symbols of the Lord Jesus Christ across every window that was visible. Each class dressed in red and white uniforms and sang songs to celebrate the love of God in all the songs with the guitarist.

Back in my classroom behind two wooden doors, lessons were taught with a class full of students singing days of the week and months in the year with the tune they chose to carry it in. History books that appeared in a light shade of purple were passed out just as red English books were. Everyone raised their hands in anticipation once a new door holder or line leader was chosen each week.

After about seven or eight hours, we are all sent down the hall to the aftercare room filled with crayons, colored pencils, dark brown tables, a mat, and a classic TV from the golden days. The black top was decorated in gray rubble with a tire filled with sand outside near the playground area. The girls played double dutch, hop scotch, and used chalk to draw whatever they wanted with the imaginations they had while the boys played football, basketball, and kickball in the small court in front of the playground. Afterwards, it was time to do homework.

Next to me the next morning sat a student that planted that bad seed with me and the others, but only because he did not receive the same support I received from his own mother. As class carried on, he hid in trash cans, under desks, and just gave our teacher a hard time. My mom acted as one of the volunteers at this private school after witnessing some of the struggles a few of the classmates had with reading and writing. My superhero came to rescue him from feeling alone as she created rhyming schemes to ensure that he retained everything he learned. From citing words, such as bat, sat, and cat to asking him what quarter after one meant on the clock across the classroom wall, she gained respect from him. Just to show her appreciation, my mom would often buy munchkins from the bakery three blocks away from us. As classmates praised me for having a great mom, her presence and involvement gave me a boost of confidence, knowing that we were great reflections of one another.

I know some kids feel embarrassed whenever their parents go up to the school to schedule conferences with teachers, volunteer, or to meet friends. I used to feel the same way, but I have learned that having a parent that is involved in your life shows you that they care. Not having an involved parent can create a lot of friction between everyone in a household and resentment from the children to the parent/ guardian. Often times, parents may say that they are too busy, they have to work, or that they are tired at the end of the day. On the contrary, this is what they signed up for so they must be held accountable for the decisions and sacrifices they make for you. Those early years of your life matter more than you probably think.

I have been fortunate enough to avoid negative peer pressure (drugs, sex, and violence). Remaining focused, staying in school, and self-improvement are some keys to being a productive member of society in my book. The father figure in my life was not a good example of how a man is and should be. I have been a great example thus far.

My relationships with my fellow relatives on his side of the family have been tarnished, too. While I was growing up, I spent my time bonding with them. From sleepovers to holiday dinners, we became close, but since he left, it seems as though they packed up and moved with him. I know it is sad, but I met new people as time passed.

As I entered into my final year at this second private school, a tragedy struck a few weeks before my 8th birthday in the spring. My loved one suffered from a stroke and was rushed to what I call her trooper room. She became a diabetic, but was neglecting herself by not taking proper care of herself emotionally, physically, psychology, or spiritually. I remember visiting her like it was yesterday.

CHAPTER FIVE

WHEN MY HEART WAS ATTACKED

My loved one fell into a diabetic coma for approximately ten days. I cried every time I went to the hospital thinking that there was hope as she laid in the coma.

We prayed and prayed enough to shake the devil away until she began to recover. Thankfully, she woke up on the day of my eighth birthday and that has been one of the best gifts in my life.

After my loved one recovered from her stroke, she needed an ample amount of time to focus on her recovery. I still did not think she understood the severity of the situation. Her health has since improved, but still has its challenges. This experience made me cry because seeing her in that state made me feel helpless, remembering how the family went to her house all the time for all the holidays and celebrations. Her house was a home, where I spent many nights as a child.

Seeing her in the hospital bed made me remember the times she drove me to church on some Sunday mornings to sit in the morning worship service in her sanctuary of worship.

Although I have faith.

It has been hard for me to comprehend how she made it through that traumatic experience. My mom and I tried to assist her even when she refused to accept help at the time. Her health continues to plateau and she has no desire to seek help.

That experience showed me that by not surrounding myself with her problems and respecting her lifestyle, I could not let it drag me down. No one is going to accept help until they are ready to accept it. It does not matter if you want to. If they do not want it, it will not happen. Focusing on positive things that are happening in your life will keep your mind off negative things that have happened. Those things cannot be changed.

After my eighth birthday, I excelled at this second private school for the last time. I almost received all A's for all four quarters during the school year on my report card. I took part in a volleyball game with the students in the elementary school class weeks before the school year ended. The game was held at a high school. We won the soccer game and won second place in the sack race across a grassy field as we were saturated in sweat and by the heat. I reluctantly joined the team not knowing what was in store for me. Nevertheless, the older students on the team and from past years gained much more respect for me. Everyone noticed how athletic I was despite my corpulent, short physical appearance, but the fact that they even noticed me gave me more self-esteem knowing that they valued my presence on the court.

CHAPTER SIX

MY SECOND PHASE

In the summers of 2007 and 2008, I was attending a summer camp at a local church between the ages of eight and nine. I had an opportunity to meet other students from around the county and outside of the county. Every day we followed a routine with a list of activities.

In the morning, we were given leisure time until it was time to eat golden pancakes, brown waffles, and a glass of orange juice for breakfast with the younger children in the church's daycare center filled with toys and coloring books to grab our attention. Then, we would walk to the building next door to practice reading, writing, and math. Recess was usually the best part of my day after we had lunch. Swinging on those yellow monkey bars, sliding down the purple tube we called a slide, and playing tag in chips made of tan colored wood relieved tons of stress for me from the rough morning. Our day would continue with a special activity we were designated to have for that specific day. Field trips, ice cream socials, and sprinkler days were other examples of events that could be held. Our day would conclude with a little more leisure time, but instead of playing cards or board games, we watched an educational video with a life lesson of some sort.

Fortunately, I was able to get along with children of all ages at the camp. They were able to reciprocate the same feelings towards me. My counselors organized a commencement exercise for all of the students at the end of the summer. We, as students, spoke about all the fun we had. I took pictures with some of the other students.

At this age, you are supposed to be at the peak of childhood. You are still wet behind the ears with innocence written all over your face. In this stage of your life, teachers seem genuine and seem to honestly care about you and your education. You get special quirks, such as not getting homework over the weekends and having holiday parties on the day before a long break from school.

It is unfortunate when people try to force you to grow up too fast and too early making decisions you are not ready to make yet. In the fall of the same year, I registered for school as a nine-year-old student. This required me to make many adjustments. All of my life, I attended private schools that followed their own curriculum.

My time at this school was life altering. This chapter of my life helped me to see teachers for who they really were. In the next chapter, you will be able to distinguish between teachers who were passionate about kids and wanted to watch them succeed and ones who were only looking for a paycheck.

CHAPTER SEVEN

DREAM TIME

Now I have reached those double digits at ten years old, a learning age, where some stuff isn't real anymore and when the realness of the world starts to kick in. This next school provided opportunities for me.

Our classes were divided into groups that consisted of colors, such as red, yellow, green, and blue. I was in the yellow group and was stuck with the same students all day every day. I made a few new friends, but then a frenemy relationship emerged. My mom would tell me that people are crazy and the older I get the more I am beginning to come to that conclusion.

When you meet someone new for the first time whether it is a male or female, they do not reveal their true colors. Once you are around them long enough, you see them for who they are. Sometimes you have to be willing to let people in your life go if they bring negativity in your life. I learned this lesson when I found out one was never really a friend to me.

Our reading, language arts, and visual arts teacher hosted an event at the school for the students. The poetry theater consisted of each student presenting all of their written work to the students. The theater was laced with black curtains that covered the promethean boards when the lights were turned off. We were given sweet tasting snacks to nibble on as we snapped our fingers after every person finished speaking their spoken words.

These poems represented topics we chose. My former friend and I collaborated on these projects and received positive feedback. I soon found out that he was a fraud. He was petty, dishonest, and just not a real friend. He eventually left the school. I never saw him again. He was "drama."

The final year of elementary school came. As top dogs, we thought we were at the top of the world. Our classes were organized in a similar fashion, but by colleges. The classes were represented by the names of colleges/universities our teachers attended.

My homeroom teacher was a good person, but had many unreasonable expectations placed on us in her class. She wanted spiral notebooks instead of loose leaf paper to write on and for us to raise our hands to answer a question she asked incoherently. As a dancer, she was skilled in many genres. From hip-hop to jazz and from ballet to Latin, she brought components of her wishy washy personality while she simultaneously showed off her lean, toned, and strong legs in her leotards.

In the same summer after my elementary school graduation, I attended the school's summer camp, where I was fortunate to learn how to do an iconic dance. It was not an easy dance, but her other students and I practiced every day with our time, effort, and consistency. The music video was approximately thirteen minutes long. The highlight of the dance performance was when we made intimidating facial expressions emulating the creatures in the music video we'd seen while the narrator spoke about what was to come in a mysterious manner. She brought me out of my condensed shell with this dance performance. She left the school in order to pursue bigger and better things.

My social studies and reading/language arts teachers were both great teachers who definitely contributed to my educational foundation just as my other teachers did. Just like the workforce, there is always at least one person you may dislike or have trouble getting along with. My elementary school math teacher was one of those people. My math teacher had his eyes set on becoming a school principal and diverted so much attention to becoming a principal that he neglected his duties as a teacher. He never wanted to assist me if I had any questions. He would barely offer coach class. My mom and I attempted to work with him extensively, but that failed after he told her, "Maybe math is just not his thing". Words cannot describe how furious my mom was and how she pictured herself wanting to jump across his wooden desk and strangle him. His arrogance made him ugly. Prior to my high school graduation, he passed away. I was informed by one of my school's former secretaries. My friends were devastated even though I was not.

My dreams of becoming a firefighter soon faded. Even though the idea of rescuing the citizens of Maryland from flames of danger dwindled away, the thought of becoming an elementary school English teacher grew stronger and stronger during this time. I considered English to be my strongest subject, a subject that allowed me to step outside of my comfort zone and open up verbally in a room with inspirational quotes and vocabulary words on the walls. I felt safe in the comfort of my social studies teacher and language arts teacher. Watching them use washable rainbow colored markers to write all the letters like a, e, i, o, u, and y we, as students, used to take notes and folk stories about legends in ancient history that we read allowed me to picture myself in a classroom with students telling them about how much they're destined to be shooting stars in the sky. Sadly, the insults outweighed the confidence builders in me when my elementary school math teacher's insults acted like little gremlins in my head that were still stealing my happiness and joy from that point on.

At my second commencement ceremony, I was recognized for my academic achievement, leadership, and perfect school attendance. For this occasion, I recall wearing a red vest with a pair of khaki pants and black shoes. It was held in the school's cafeteria in elementary school. I attended an after school program and started to invest my energy into playing the recorder and taking karate lessons. The last memory I have from being in elementary school was the yearbook, where my friend and I were chosen for the friendliest boy and girl.

This chapter in my life taught that me that it is imperative that you choose your friends wisely and that you have to cherish the relationship you have with them. Everyone who speaks to you, everyone you may surround yourself with, and everyone who grins in your face is not considered a friend or a great support system. If you truly want to know whether or not that person is genuine, check to see how they interact with you when others are not around. Are they supportive and encouraging? Do they help you when you are feeling blue? Do you have anything in common with this person? Are they self-centered? Do they bring negativity? After answering these questions, I was able to create a different perception about those kinds of people. I know I have. Overall, I have done a good job choosing my friends. I needed to exclude certain people from my circle because of the type of energy they brought to me. Do not be afraid to do it yourselves. Sometimes it is for the best.

In addition to choosing your friends wisely, this chapter also taught me how to ignore naysayers. In school, growing up, I struggled with many rigorous mathematics courses and my level of confidence would shatter every time I entered into a class with an impatient, smart-mouthed math teacher. Nevertheless, I continued to work hard on home assignments and class assignments in spite of the failing grades I may have received on any assessments. As my mom always says, 'hard work pays off". A hard-working student brings much more effort and success than a student who is a good test-taker.

Before I started middle school, my friends and I noticed many changes that began to happen within the school and ourselves. Many people transferred to magnet schools from around town, teachers moved, or continued to teach the same grades. The onset of puberty was about to begin. I was now involved in other extracurricular activities outside of school, but in the next stage of my life, I began to struggle with my body image and food addiction and having irritating and discouraging instructors and salty teachers did not help.

CHAPTER EIGHT

MY SAPPY SOUP SONG

In the middle school, I expected things to be different for me. In some ways, it was, but in other ways, it was not. Even though I was well dressed in a white collared shirt, navy blue pants, black shoes, and a dark blue vest, I continued to feel the same inside and out. I had one of the meanest and nastiest teachers this year. We had the grouch in the morning for reading, which is where she covered a wide variety of subjects. She was known for giving out weekly book reports, journal entries, and drills with giggles as she fed her face with chocolate, powder covered, and cream filled doughnuts. In the midst of loading us up with work, she was hot-tempered, rude, very unprofessional, and left me paranoid in her position of authority.

After a few conferences with my mother, this grouch with a mean streak made a slight attitude adjustment. Her disgusting attitude had no place in a school with future leaders.

The beginning of middle school was rough for me after many of my insecurities started to kick in. People made sly remarks about my body image and frustrations with wanting to excel in any and everything is what I became eager to pursue. Juggling my schoolwork, social life, and extra curricular activities stressed me out at times. As a result, I began to turn to food for comfort instead of drugs and alcohol. Although, food in a sense, did act as a drug because it provided me with a momentary fulfillment. This gradually continued into the next year of middle school. I started to pack on pounds every month of each year. It hindered me from displaying any type of self-confidence.

After I decided to enroll in an after school program at a local studio in middle school, I spent all three years of middle school in this program while I simultaneously learned how to play an instrument, the recorder. Being involved in these activities gave me discipline and ways to stay active. However, an unnecessary amount of stress and pressure was placed on me in order to reach and achieve perfection even though my mom always taught me to honor my commitments academically, scholastically, and athletically in addition to doing my best.

At the studio, I participated in many self-defense classes with instructors of all ages. The program had a few drivers who picked us up from school and opened the glass doors to a place that was painted in dark blue and white colors with the male and female dressing rooms installed in the middle of the floor. The counselors helped us with our homework before snack time.

My peers and I spent an hour learning various techniques each evening in a white Gi and bare feet. The Wednesday sparring lessons gave me an opportunity to release tension I kept inside. One of the instructors was packed with comic relief and strived for a healthy lifestyle.

Along with his passion, patience, and optimism, he taught me how to swim in a pool filled with light blue chlorine after I attended summer camp at the same studio. Two other instructors in particular always brought that tough, but fun-filled energy, while serving as the voice of reason, bringing sweet, tender energy. My mom was there to support me during my testing sessions for the next belt.

Nevertheless, I was able to enhance my skills in karate through this program at the studio. I made it to the advanced green belt by the time I graduated from middle school. I withered from playing the recorder, too.

CHAPTER NINE

CHURCH BELLS

Another sentimental moment was being baptized at a young age by a church leader. I have been attending the same church for almost twenty years. In middle school, I joined the money board. The duties of this position require a lot more than what people typically think. Some of those responsibilities include keeping track of who uses the facility, paying for the utilities, and calculating the total amount of money collected after each worship service ends.

In my opinion, the position has not really been difficult to manage, but it may be because I abide by the rules that coincide with the position. I also joined the kindness ministry. In this ministry, we provide goods and services to people in need and check on people who are sick and shut in. The members of the congregation have watched me grow up.

Some of them have had positive influences on me and the decisions I have made in my life because regardless of what is believed to be true or untrue, having a role model in your life helps you to focus and never lose sight of what is important.

Most of my role models influenced me by being practical, passionate, and humble. Whether they have attended college, joined the military, or entered the workforce. It all came as a level of success for each of them.

CHAPTER TEN

CHURCH BELLS: REFLECTIONS

On the contrary, one thing that a church can lack is the commitment from its members. A church primarily consists of approximately or at least close to a descent amount of members, in my opinion, with 70% of them being women and 30% of them being men. Some churches currently have sprinkles of kids/young adults remaining. The older members of the population are elderly, ill, retired, disabled, and are sometimes limited in their abilities to perform certain tasks in the congregation, but there are times when I get the feeling that these members do not care about the church as they claim.

An aging congregation leads to a dying church, which is what I fear as years go by. In one ear and out the other, a wolf pack of one stands front and center when it becomes a ghost town on Sundays between those maroon colored chairs and white washed walls. On Sunday morning, sitting in a little corner next to an exit door to a church with the red holy bible in my paws, I listen to God's sermon instead of his child preaching the sermon.

Although humble and loving, sometimes unassertive and unappreciative are other words that describe the ones who sometimes take hard working, committed members for granted as they cater to the fickle ones by sending them prayer requests and covenants for communion on communion Sunday.

All the bathrooms that have been cleaned, all the precious time that's been wasted, all of the love that was missed, and all of the ungodly vibes that were given off by a few members of the church body leave me with a broken heart remembering how you can begin with tons of members in the beginning and how it's been watered down to having less.

"I don't marry every couple!", "Those racists folks", "back in my day", "Young people don't know nothing about good music nowadays," and "when I was a child "are common words that may be stated from a baby boomer during their Sunday school sermons, studies, or lessons.

These remarks leave me with a bitter taste in my mouth and feelings of disappointment for feeling unwanted in a congregation filled with a "children/young people should be seen and not heard" mentality. It is a reminder of how ethnically and culturally diverse my sets of friends are and how the world is now for a millennial and babies born after the year Y2K .

Telling me until I am blue in the face about blessing young people like myself and accepting them for who they are, but contradicting themselves as they continue to keep a close mind instead of an open one. The more I attend worship, the more I see what is under the surface of everyone's smile.

A morning service is conducted every Sunday. In the midst of having friendly fellowship, the creator of the bulletins told me, "you're too skinny, you don't need to lose anymore weight." In her eyes, it appeared as though I dismissed her insults, but my mom and I were uncomfortable with her for throwing shade even though it appeared as though she wasn't trying hard to keep a great shape.

By sticking together, we can all make a difference for the next generations. Now that I am a young adult, it bothers me when the people call my mom and I, "Lisa -Nelson", as if we are the same person and not individuals. Not to say that I am ashamed of her being my mom because I am not, I love her. I would not trade her for any other, but my question to them would be, 'Who am I to you when she is not present?'. 'Who is she to you when I am not present?' She has a story to tell and so do I, but it is not the same story. We are close, but we are two separate people. Now that I am older, I hope people treat me as the young adult-I am. I am unique. I am the future.

CHAPTER ELEVEN

GORGEOUS GIRLS & THEIR BOISTEROUS BOYS

In the fall of the year, 2011, was a year that did not come with as many adjustments. I was twelve and one-year shy of being a teenager, but I continued to run to food for comfort in order to cope with stress. Within the yellow and brown colored walls surrounded by the blue metal lockers near the school library, I had encounters with the new school bully who started to smell his own pee and my first crush, a new student in my class. This year definitely came with new surprises.

My first love and first crush came to our charter school after transferring from another elementary school. Her caramel skin, wavy black hair, squeaky voice, and crystal clear glasses intrigued me the most out of all. The two of us befriended each other after having some of the same classes. She and I had similar hobbies and interests, which is how we connected. The two of the most sentimental and unforgettable moments we spent together were at an annual get together event for a special visit by a local radio station to meet a popular girl group. We held great conversations; however, there were other suitors.

The middle school's miniskirt chaser came strutting by with his chocolate skin, six pack abs, and obnoxious persona. All the girls fell head over heels for him, even the one I adored. I secretively witnessed her having her first kiss with her chocolate thunder in the school hallway. I can admit that I was heartbroken because I wanted to be her first kiss. My crush lasted until the end of middle school before graduation. Although I was fearful of rejection, I eventually confessed my feelings to her. She was surprised, but not at all disgusted with what I had to say. She appreciated me caring about her so much. We remained friends until the two of us graduated and went our separate ways. I have not seen her since. My fear of rejection came from the insecurities I had about my physical appearance. I was not tall, buff, muscular, or even the same complexion as the boys who seemed to be considered attractive. My insecurities about my physical appearance created emptiness inside of me and displayed my self-doubt on the outside.

The middle school bully was a part of our school family since the very beginning. For some reason, he thought that he was the big cheese because of his stature and social status in school. I continued to avoid him at all costs, but he was not the only one bullying other students. His friends made constant attempts to emulate him.

Their childish antics became a running gag throughout the three years of middle school. Jumping on desks as soon as the teacher left the room, using profanity to impress the pretty chicks, and bullying the people they thought they were bigger and more important than were examples.

As you go through various stages of your life, you are, at times, so anxious to escape and leave that phase. I am not sure about you, but every now and then, I feel nostalgic enough to take a trip down memory lane. You never know when you may bump into people you have encountered in the past. They may end up in a good predicament or a bad one. It is sufficed to say that middle school can be rough and wild. From going through puberty to trying to confront bullies or even having your first kiss, middle school comes with many physical, emotional, and psychological changes.

CHAPTER TWELVE

HOW TABLES TURN

"You need to value the importance of having relatives and friends in your corner," people in my life always say. Many people go through trials and tribulations alone because they are too prideful to seek help. I used to be afraid to seek help because I viewed it as a weakness. My mom told me repeatedly, "the stupid question is the one you do not ask". In my last year of middle school, I found that out.

The last year of middle school came around. Words cannot describe how happy I was to leave at the time. I was sick of middle school in its entirety. However, I did receive an enormous amount of assistance. I received assistance from two teachers in middle school that have mathematics and reading credentials.

One of the reading teachers in my final days of middle school taught a class of mine that consisted of myself and two other students. I would describe her as being resourceful and knowledgeable. She served as my voice-of-reason once I was able to discuss personal struggles and issues with her. I knew that she would provide me with a good listening ear. She wore dresses down to her ankles,chewed bubble gum, and wiggled her toes through her open toed shoes. She had adapted to an older method of teaching with her use of flash cards, games, and other techniques as she gathered a few of us in the corner of the library every day. She was determined to shape me into becoming a better reader and better writer. Now, the both of us are proud. My reading teacher retired after teaching students for a few more years. If I saw her again, I would thank her for molding me into the reader and writer I am today. The beauty in this teacher came from her persistence and passion for teaching and being the best educator possible.

On the other hand, my middle school math teacher did not initially give the best welcoming or warm response. Other students from previous years made her out to be a monster because of her teaching style and snarky personality. Time after time, I attended coach class for assistance, but it was still difficult for me to comprehend anything. I was afraid of flunking that class. After a while, her teaching style matured as she continued to mold and perfect her craft. The beauty in her developed as she started to open up and display an alternative side to her gift in teaching mathematics.

Playing soccer on Sunday afternoons with an ethnically diverse set of teammates gave me an outlet and was exciting. Each Sunday, the players would meet in a high school gymnasium. The teams were split into colors: red, white, blue, and purple. Two teams faced each other every week for about two hours and the season lasted from January until the end of March.

My teammates consistently praised me for putting forth my best effort in every game. Kicking the ball, blocking the goals, and stealing the ball from my opponents across the field for my team brought great vibes from adults on the bleachers who were surprised that a kid weighing over 200lbs and standing a little over five feet could be a great player. An awards ceremony was held in the school's cafeteria in April of the same year. I was awarded two trophies for my participation and for being the most valuable player. I appreciated all of the praise I received from everyone.

My middle school graduation was held in the auditorium. At the ceremony, I was recognized for maintaining perfect attendance and making great progress in reading. The ceremony lasted for about two hours. I said my final goodbyes to my elementary and middle school friends. My classmates and I spent our last moments together at our trip to a museum in Virginia and at our end of school cookout. I had the privilege to serve on the yearbook committee this year and photographed everything that took place. Not to mention that I was chosen to as one of the leaders of my school's Safety Patrol group, where I instructed the elementary school students in the safest possible way. For my efforts, free tickets to attend a sports game.

Before the graduation ceremony ended, we all found out

which schools we were attending for high school. My desire to dive deeper into science became a new career path. I was accepted after scoring 80 points on my placement exam to a high school entering into the Environmental Science program.

This part of my life taught me how to capture sentimental moments in a photograph whenever I get the chance. When I received my first yearbook, I was excited to be one of the students to graduate from the very first graduating middle school class from the charter school, knowing that I was one of the key members of the yearbook committee for the entire year. My feelings of excitement soon ended once I realized that I was not featured in the photograph with the other members of the committee.

I remembered that I had refused to take a picture with the other members because I felt uncomfortable displaying my overweight, unhealthy body across the pages in the yearbook. At the time, I thought that it made no difference because readers would be able to see my name on the list with the members in the yearbook, but what really made the difference was not savoring the memories. Now that I look back, I wish I would have taken that picture with my peers and not cared so much about feeling embarrassed in the eyes of them, but another person made me feel even worse about my self-image.

Later one night, in a popular restaurant in town, a tall, middle-aged coach from a city school approached my mother and I at dinner. He asked me if I played football. He kept making statements over and over again about how a boy my size would win championships for his team, how a boy my size needed to stay my size, and how a boy my size would win scholarships to any college. I used my smile as a mask to hide behind the sadness I felt after he finished those statements.

The next chapter of our lives began, my low self-confidence and self-esteem continued. My insecurities about my body image reached their peak after I tried to wear clothes that could not fit. I felt so discouraged while I was shopping for new clothes in a store for the next school year.

As I stood there in the dressing room filled with mirrors and used hangers, I hear a gentleman telling my mom, "he's going to lose all that weight, you'll see". I soon felt exposed and suicidal afterwards. I assumed that my physical appearance was what everyone was concerned about. Sneaking food was my comfort just like a child with a blanket. Everyone young and old would give me backhanded compliments about my size.

Going to the doctor's office for my next visit left me feeling guilty, as my mom looked clueless with tears in her eyes knowing her little boy was in trouble. She did not know what to do next. My doctor looked at the two of us in disgust and disappointment as he flips through his paperwork. People would make comments, such as "He is adorable, but he is a little fat". You are a big boy! Do you play football?" The more I heard those sly remarks, the more ashamed and embarrassed I felt. The beginning of my high school life became a disaster as I fell into a deep state of depression. None of my achievements from the past mattered anymore. At the age of fourteen, I decided to become an overachiever and overcompensated with school because I felt unattractive and unworthy. I was uncomfortable with the heavyset ninth grader that weighed 236lbs at the age of fourteen.

CHAPTER THIRTEEN

THE PIT OF DESPAIR: FRESHMAN BLUES

In August of 2013, I entered high school on a Monday into three sets of doors with a list of eight classes that were divided into an A day and B day schedule. Adjusting to a new environment filled with older students intimidated me. My classmates and I were new to everything from teachers to students and from clubs to sports. Even though the school only had a student-faculty ratio of 20:1, give or take a few, some of us still had a difficult time locating the rooms where our classes were held. I was scheduled to have PE as a first period class on "A" days for the entire year. My class consisted of three arrogant and obnoxious student aides, who teased and taunted the freshmen in the class who ran laps around the gym filled with dark blue bleachers that covered white, light blue, and black colors on the mascot's face that was pasted on every corner.

After spending months and months isolating myself from everyone, I turned to food in order to cope with stress. I was overwhelmed with the workload from each individual class, but I was even more overwhelmed with having a condescending math teacher and an authoritative, demanding, and unreasonable social studies teacher. I was fortunate enough to make it through, but it was not easy.

A high school math class was a class I chose to drop from my schedule that year. He was even worse than my elementary school math teacher. It is almost as if he enjoyed watching his students struggle. This teacher gave the class a descent amount of work, but placed many unrealistic expectations on us in regards to how much information we were supposed to know or understand from each lesson. I was too paranoid to confront him in the beginning, but as time passed, I expressed to him my reasons for not wanting to continue taking his course in the nicest, most respectful way I could. I tried to give him the benefit of the doubt, but I dropped another class he taught in the year because I refused to suffer in silence again.

In spite of it all, I did manage to have two great math teachers throughout my years in high school. They offered coach class before school and after school, kept positive attitudes, and gave me the grades I deserved for all of my hard work and effort. Sadly, that math teacher moved away and the other math teacher ended his teaching career and took time to travel. I am glad I was given the opportunity to learn new and everlasting math skills from them. Their classrooms were almost like safe havens for me because I was not afraid to ask questions I wanted or needed to ask or participate whenever I was called on to answer a question. The beauty in both of these men came from their uplifting, optimistic attitudes.

For social studies classes, this manic teacher was a fireball of a woman and a tall piece of work in the beginning. Her lessons were taught at a fast pace every period. She gave us at least ten handouts filled with US amendments, bills of rights, and supreme court cases for a quiz she intended to give us in the upcoming week. I still remember sitting in this teacher's classroom at back to school night with the expression of fear written on my face as I left her classroom and drove in the car with my mom home.

My high school was known for being one of the best magnet high schools in the county, state, and nation. The curriculum was much more challenging than ones at other high schools. My anxiety and stress was bottled up for a long period of time. I was tired of feeling inadequate. My grades never satisfied me even though my mom thought so. I became very resistant about participating in any sports, clubs, or organizations and continued to turn to food as an outlet in order to cope with my emotions I internalized. In the middle of my freshman year, my mom decided to take me to a doctor once I felt as though a change needed to be made.

I soon signed up for sessions at a private practice with a doctor. Every evening, a few times a week, we would spend about an hour discussing many of my typical teenage problems in his office filled with soft cushioned chairs. He gave me many tools and techniques to use that I have never used before. I noticed that he was very perceptive and a great listener. After the session ended, he would bring my mom back to his office and discuss what I wanted him to discuss with her. Thankfully, he respected my wishes after I answered a list of questions he began to ask me.

"What is your biggest fear about…?"
"Have you ever thought of…...?"
"What is your relationship like with…?"
"If you do this, then maybe…?"

After a couple of months, I decided that it was time to take the training wheels off and branch out on my own. I felt as though it was time to put those strategies I had learned to the test. I started to bond with classmates, but remained cautious.

One of my teachers, I considered a self-improvement teacher. I was a part of a class which promoted college readiness and enhanced the necessary skills that are needed to be successful in the workforce. I was enrolled in that course through a random lottery selection process and interview. I enjoyed the time I spent in that class and she never failed to mention to me how much I have progressed over the years.

A counselor played the same role, but as more of a motherly figure to me because she served as my voice-of-reason with her kind, nurturing spirit. Having her as a support system contributed to my success.

One teacher, I considered as a mentor to me. I was introduced to her on my first day of the year in my second class. I was definitely reserved, but I had the opportunity to witness her cheerful and easygoing personality in a classroom filled with fish, beige colored stoops, microscopes, and periodic tables. She helped me get rid of my perfectionist ways. She even asked to me to consider joining the running team after my sophomore year ended, which I accepted. My team and I ran great races through the rocky valleys, steep hills, and thorny bushes. There were moments when I struggled athletically and scholastically, but I could always go to the coach for help.

Unlike many other teachers, she never misjudged me and always tried to develop a better understanding of whatever issue I had. She wrote many letters of recommendations for me and spoke of me in a positive light. I appreciated all the insight she has given me, too. I hope she remembers me as a role model and inspiration to students who struggle with body image and self-acceptance. A year later, I landed an internship with a government agency in the beginning of my senior year. I thanked her for her enthusiasm and integrity that made her beautiful personality shine.

Later that summer, riding along in the passenger seat in my mom's red truck, I saw a sign that requested boys for a football camp that was taking place. I immediately thought about me at my weight even though I agreed to participate. It did not take much for rudeness to pollute the air I absorbed when the first day of camp came. Tackling dummies, lifting my bodyweight up off the ground, and running laps around the green field was painful. No breaks, sympathy, or favors were given. The relentless amount of time I spent practicing meant nothing as they continued to funk up my spirit with their biceps, triceps, six pack abs, and brassy attitudes as they shamed me away before my mom and I called it quits.

On July 24, 2014, the bright sunny, summer day was a day that lightened my mood. I was tired of living in an unhealthy and miserable frame of mind. For years, I spent the majority of time using food to cope with emotions I could not tolerate, leaving me depressed whenever I felt lonely. I woke up and ran upstairs. I asked my mom for help on how to lose weight. I wanted to try something different. That day was the day I chose to live a healthier and happier lifestyle through proper diets and sufficient amounts of exercise.

CHAPTER FOURTEEN

THE UNDISCOVERED DISCOVERIES

One hobby that I developed an interest in high school was writing while I was going through the transition of losing weight and adapting to a healthier and happier lifestyle. Ever since I was fourteen, I have been writing about my personal life and many struggles that I have or the struggles I have witnessed other people have. I have since written and composed many songs and poems with a wide variety of topics ranging from love, heartbreak, self-improvement, male empowerment, family, and friends. My passion for music factors into my love for writing because it creates an outlet for me when I have a difficult time expressing myself verbally to others. Now that I am older, I continue to learn more about myself more and more. I sometimes look back at some of the things I talked about in my writing in the beginning of high school just to see how much I have matured. I now write about ways I could handle issues within my community, such as crime and colorism.

Music runs in parts of my family. I would consider myself a music buff because of the amount of music I listen to and the number of musicians and artists I admire and listen to from all genres. Music is also my stress-reliever and helps me cope with internal issues I have. Music is a part of the reason why I sing on the male chorus at my church and why I share my weight loss story to children, teens, and young adults. From rhythm and blues to pop, from country to rock and roll to even rap, I have a list of musical icons from many generations.

In the R&B and rap world, I would consider most of the artists to be my musical influences because of how dynamic they are with their work. They all have been around for decades combining various elements of music to express themselves. This genre of music combines old school soul and spoken word. Female artists use their femininity through their music and their voices. You have musicians that are legendary in the older days of music and are well respected in the business and ones that march to the beats of their own drums with their stylish clothes and vocals that expand in any and every range. I recall seeing one for the first time in a concert for my tenth birthday. My eyes almost bulged out of my head when I watched her perform live. Words cannot describe how much I enjoyed myself.

Unlike other cliché rappers, some express themselves and vocalize their talents by talking about their upbringings. They have made their marks in this industry and have expanded their brand outside of music. Some trending artists are known as gospel rappers for my generation. They are philanthropists and activists. By donating money to hometowns and school systems, they act as role models for so many young people, including myself. I see a brighter future for these superstars.

The country-pop music world consists of artists that bring a unique sound compared to the other music I listen to. This genre of music tells stories about their lives and where life, in general, is headed. Some are known for their belting techniques in their music and have voices that pierce through you like a sword when you hear it. I love girl groups filled with diverse sets of members ethnically, vocally, and physically. They often harmonize and add their own individual flavors to the group. Many solo artists discuss pop-culture and various lifestyles (relationships, self-empowerment, etc.) in their music. Others play many instruments, something I have never thought of before.

I am known for composing narratives about my personal life like other artists I love. They are a part of the reason they're role models and inspirations for my written work and me. They have made many accomplishments as young people and are never afraid to be as authentic as possible in a song. I hope they stick around and continue to inspire others in generations to come.

There are other vocal groups I enjoy listening to and other solo acts I love, but the list goes on for days. The bottom line is that I am so musically inclined that I listen to just about any type. Some of the best dancers I have seen in my time are the ones I have seen in television shows, movies, and all through the media. I love the way they feel the music whenever they have the chance to perform. I watch and listen to them. I am sure you do, too.

I have to admit, listening to gospel music soothes my soul sometimes, especially when I am having a bad day. Gospel music is inspirational and motivating music for me. Combining today's music with the older rhythms make the sound even more appealing to any audience.

Fitness idols and body activists in the media inspire me to do what I do. They are not ashamed of who they are and are passionate about making this world a better place through health and wellness. We are all sending the same message.

Reading, writing, and singing got me through many of my growing pains I had in high school and is still an outlet for me today. At the age of seventeen, at the end of my senior year, I began drawing. I became interested in this after my art teacher told us to draw characters from cartoons between generations of animated television. I record the dates by weeks just as I record my age after I finish writing to see the amount of progress I have made. Even though fitness comes first, I still take time out of my busy schedule to invest in this. I am now incorporating some of my own illustrations with my artwork.

After taking a test to determine my real ethnicity, I found out that I was not African American at all, but I was of Polynesian, Native American, Caucasian, and African descent.

To be honest, I never thought that I was purely one race, which is why I wanted to dig deeper to figure out where my roots come from. At first, I guessed, thinking I was Caucasian and Mexican/Dominican/Puerto Rican, but I was wrong. That goes to show you that you never know how far your roots go back. Just like my weight, I have received backhanded remarks about my skin from people with similar ethnic backgrounds as well. Let us embrace everyone for who they are and what they are without casting judgment. Just give yourself a chance to get to know them. Gay, straight, black, white, or whatever the case may be. Being prejudice is a thing in the past, so leave it there! I have managed to show that by surrounding myself with all types of people.

CHAPTER FIFTEEN

MEMORY BOOK

I call this chapter, "Memory Book", because you will read about my high school friends, the good times we have had, and learn about the positive young people I have surrounded myself with, the people who push me to work harder to achieve my goals and to live my dreams.

There were students I collaborated with frequently during my high school years. However, one of them had tons of history with me. In elementary school, we attended the same school, but he carried himself in a completely different manner. He was actually very snobbish and self-absorbed running around in his football uniform being chased by classmates in duck duck goose. I kept my distance from him as much as possible.

In high school, he had more of an outgoing and easygoing personality. The beauty in him came from humbling himself gradually realizing that he didn't have to be thirsty like a desert for attention and that he could just be himself. The two of us have become close friends since the beginning of high school and we still communicate with each other from time to time. The others came from various backgrounds. One was a Spanish sensation. She befriended me in a math class filled with irrational equations, graphs, and incoherent word problems. Her tan skin, dark hair, light brown eyes, and full figured, curvy figure allowed me to see her unconventional beauty and personality that was similar to mine- perfectionism. She hated making mistakes and feeling like the center of embarrassment in class.

At our senior prom, we hung out together looking like a Hollywood couple walking down the red carpet. Her magnet program was centered around flipping burgers, wearing aprons, and protecting her high maintenance manicures and pedicures with gloves. The beauty in her as a Latin princess comes from learning from her own mistakes and not looking at them as weaknesses.

The only female student in a magnet program centered around wheels, oil, gas, breaks, and engines befriended me in the beginning of high school. She was active in clubs and sports. From using her light bulb in the NHS and Robotics Club-tearing opponents apart with her talents and skills on the basketball team and lacrosse team.

As her beauty continues to smile through her pearly whites, she continues to remind me of how the two of us continue to climb ladders, break down walls, and honor our words as lifelong Christians. The beauty in her comes from her being a great listener and bringing positive energy into any poisoned atmosphere.

I also joined the Green Club and Robotics Club. These were also big steps for me. I was really beginning to come out of my shell and bond with people.

A former friend was one I met in the green club through a mutual, artistic friend. The former friend was my comic relief, voice-of-reason, and provided enthusiasm whenever I was down. She was in touch with her faith and to honor the hijab she wore against her pretty cafe colored skin, I told her that I appreciated the friendship and loyalty as my friend. This modeled her beauty.

The running star is another girl I met during my junior year. She was a very gorgeous girl. Her wavy hair, wide smile, chocolate skin, and athletic built stood out from the other girls in my eyes. The nerdy kid loses again when he finds out that the chocolate hunk with the six pack abs gets the girl he likes. It felt like a repeat of my experience with my middle school crush at sixteen years old instead of twelve years old.

I congratulated her for her accomplishments even though I missed the chance of having the chance to identify the beauty in her on the inside as much as the outside.

I met the visual artist right after I met the free spirit in the green club, too. I would describe the visual artist as being very nonchalant and carefree about most things whenever she walked into our green room with flower pots, soil, and seeds.

She has an environmentally friendly personality to match her delicious vanilla flavored skin and her strands of hair were dyed in every color of the rainbow. She is the one that inspired me to practice visual art. Whenever she picked up a pen, paintbrush, charcoal, a piece of paper, or anything, she would express her free-spirited personality through her artwork. Her beauty shined through her independence, nonconformist attitude, and creative mindset as the gifted ivory lady.

My tenure at my magnet school would not have been great without the support and encouragement from a loyal set of ethnically and culturally diverse friends. It took me a while to step outside of my comfort zone, but I have savored all the moments.

CHAPTER SIXTEEN

MOMENTS THAT LAST FOREVER

In the midst of handling core courses, I took advantage of the opportunity to visit a science center and a zoo. We conducted research and experiments with our teachers. Everything I learned and the information I retained was not only interesting, but also fulfilling for me. I graded these teachers' beauty through their work as environmentalists.

I also had taken a social science course. In that class, we took a series of tests, watched movies, and discovered many things about ourselves. I had the chance to see this teacher display his true colors. In the beginning, he portrayed himself as being sophisticated. This slim brunette with a tucked in shirt and tie gradually became patronizing through his put downs and brazen remarks. I can only hope that he has humbled himself as I did that summer volunteering at a senior center at the age of sixteen. The director gave me a chance and gave the older generation a chance to witness 'positive' youthfulness.

I was able to lose 70lbs in one year and I trained for two and a half months to prepare for the upcoming running season.

The training was worth it and paid off after my teammates and I ran successful races for the entire season from 3Ks to 5Ks to 8Ks up and down high hills, by the end of the season, I set a personal record of 21:45. I was awarded the "Better Late Than Never Award" for running varsity as a first year runner as a junior.

Devoting my time to the green club and the robotics club had its quirks and rewards. My knowledge in the world of science increased and we made a difference. Raising money, recycling, you name it, and we have done it! I hope my hometown school system invests money in their budget to keep green clubs active.

Becoming a student aid for the school's library and a student aid for the school's program for autistic children in art class was the highlight of my final year. These duties required me to place books in numerical and chronological order, assist the students that needed help with their arts/crafts, keep track of the laptops, and laminate papers for the teachers. Watching the students blossom like flowers and mature melted my heart with joy. The teachers signed my yearbook with a message wishing me the best success in the future.

At my celebration, my colleagues, relatives, and friends came out to support me. My celebration had close to one-hundred people, a caterer to serve delicious food, a photographer to take stunning pictures, and a DJ to play awesome music. Family members and friends gave me special tributes through their poetry and words of wisdom. One of the members from the male vocal group at my church gave me a special tribute with his band's mini concert. Everyone brought all kinds of gifts. My friends and I had our own table to socialize. A church leader and his wife made a heartfelt speech while my family members created a blissful dance performance. My moms' friends helped her with the decorations. The hall was covered in green and white balloons, tablecloths, and confetti strips. I thanked everyone who came to celebrate with me.

The senior prom was and has been the greatest experience from high school. It was held at a stadium. My friends and I dressed to impress as we mingled and danced the night away. The day was somewhat hectic due to the number of senior events on the same day. On our last day, before the day was over, my mom threw a pre-prom party for me immediately after I left work and school early and invited everyone she could. Back at the junior prom, looking snazzy, with a bright orange colored collared shirt and a forest green suit jacket,I isolated myself. I watched as everyone else was having fun with his or her date. I cried after the night ended, but a year later, at the senior prom,I finally had enough courage to let go after riding in a slender, spacey limo. I had fun in my classy and not trashy attire.

Throughout the years, I was so tense, caring about everyone staring at me and judging me based off my physical appearance. It was time for me to enjoy myself. I danced the dance I have never danced before up and down that dance floor. After the night was over, I stayed up thinking about all the fun I had at my senior prom.

At the awards ceremony, families were gathered as invited students were honored with awards or scholarships for their accomplishments made for the past four years. My mom, my supervisor, and members of my church family came out to support me. There were lists of awards I won for my hard work in school, church, and at work. I received awards for perfect school attendance, (K-12), volunteer service,academic achievement, and athletic achievement.

My other friends and classmates were acknowledged for their achievements as well. We all congratulated each other.

The high school graduation was held in an arena. My senior class heard opening speeches and closing speeches given by our valedictorian,our salutatorian, our superintendent, our principals, and other county officials. We were dressed in blue and white gowns with multicolored tassels. The people I invited took pictures of me before and after the graduation ceremony. My relatives and I celebrated at a local diner to talk about my plans for my future.

CHAPTER SEVENTEEN

REFLECTIONS OF MY SOUL

There you have it. These chapters recollect the phases of my life I lived through for the past eighteen years. I was involved in activities. I became an all-a-rounder, playing sports, playing instruments, going to summer camps, and just making the most my childhood that I know I will never get back.

Discovering me and reaching self-acceptance was difficult for me to do in my middle and high school years. Struggling with my body image took its toll, but adapting to a healthier, happier lifestyle made it all worthwhile. Developing healthy ways to channel my frustrations taught me how to love, respect, and express myself. I never had any disciplinary issues, but I did have emotional issues and growing pains I did not know how to handle. I do not experiment with drugs or use drugs because I am trying my best to promote healthy living through my actions. Setting an example for the younger generations and ones to come will help make communities around the world better places to live.

That is why I have started to pursue a career as an activist, philanthropist, humanitarian, writer/poet, and artist. I want to raise awareness and promote positive aspects of topics related to colorism, beauty, body image, and self-acceptance to children, teens, and young adults. I hate to see others suffer the way I did. My story is intended to inspire and teach you how to love yourself unconditionally.

My songs, poetry, and artwork represent who I am, what I have experienced, and what I think should be incorporated into a community that is broken. My written work was introduced in the middle of 9th grade and has continued through the 12th grade. I am still writing and I will continue. Male empowerment, self-improvement, love, heartbreak, family, and friends are the range of topics I discuss.

Despite all I have been through, I still believe I am not handsome, cute, good-looking, or whatever you want to call it in a physical sense. However, I have learned that humility, taking care of myself, having a supportive family, supportive friends, and giving back identifies my true beauty. I hope that sharing my experiences with you helps you identity the beauty in you.

ABOUT THE AUTHOR

Nelson E. Brown is an Environmental Science student at the Community College of Baltimore County in Catonsville, Maryland, where he serves as one of the writers, artists, and editors of the school's literary magazine and a participant in the Project Sparks program. He's been recognized as an avid volunteer and athlete locally and nationally. In addition to being a part-time student, he is employed at the Maryland Department of the Environment as an Office Clerk, with plans of obtaining a career in Environmental Science after he finishes school. He currently resides in Randallstown, Maryland.

Made in the USA
Columbia, SC
08 September 2018